Foreword

This is a book cooked in the crucible of life. I have watched God's servant, Akinwale Babatunde, lovingly pay the price to deliver this priceless, liberating timely prophetic truth, mostly hidden from people who are devoted to a lifestyle of selflessness and Christ-likeness. This is a book that Satan dreads for you to read. The Enemy Within is light to those who are in the darkness of despair. It's medicine for the loving or wounded hearts. A trusted safety road map for all who have been ensnared in the jungle of wickedness. This is a book that everyone will one day read, better now than later.

Dr Bernard Blessing
Rescue Life International

Overcoming The Enemy Within

Wale Babatunde

Overcoming The Enemy Within

Identifying, exposing and dealing with Destiny Aborters

CHRISTIAN HERITAGE PUBLICATIONS
Overcoming The Enemy Within
Copyright©2011 by Wale Babatunde
published by
Christian Heritage Publications
25 – 27 Ruby Street
London, SE15 1LR

Unless otherwise stated, all scripture quotations are taken from the King James Version (KJV) of the Bible.

Other Versions:

Amplified Version (AMP), New American Standard Bible(NASB), New International Version (NIV), King James, 2000 Bible, New King James Version (NKJV), New Living Translation (NLT), Good News Bible (GNB), American King James Version (AKJV), New American Standard Bible (NASB), **Knox Translation of the Vulgate (Knox), An American Translation (AAT), God'S Word Translation (GWT), World English Bible (WEB)**

All rights reserved under International Copyright Law. Contents and/or cover may not be reproduced in whole or in part without the express written consent of the publisher.

"Overcoming the Enemy Within" is a must-read for those facing relational challenges and personal difficulties who wish to address the root causes of some of these challenges. Rev Babatunde identifies enemies within and without that we all face at some point in our lives, and then insightfully instructs us on how to address and overcome those enemies."

        Pastor Joseph Boadu
        Senior Pastor Christian Life Ministries,
        London

What a book! ………. No one has the knowledge and wisdom to deliver such masterpiece without the leading of the Holy Ghost so Baba, I say a big congratulations.!

A Linguistically sound, morally deep and spiritually inspiring piece of work.

        Seyi George Olofinjana,
        Hull city football club,
        Nigerian international

It is a joy to have known Pastor Wale Babatunde for the past few years as he brightens up every heart in our church with his timely and prophetic messages and revelations from the throne of grace. I have known Pastor Wale as a man of integrity, sincerity and deep rooted love for God and His church. His contributions to the body of Christ and to the Middle East churches is remarkable. Every time he comes out with a master piece from the heart of God. Overcoming the enemy within is an end time tool that the Holy Spirit has released to this generation for revival. You will be blessed by this book.

Apostle Alias
The Apostolic Ministries International
United Arab Emirates

This is a book cooked in the crucible of life. I have watched God's servant, Akinwale Babatunde, lovingly pay the price to deliver this priceless, liberating timely prophetic truth, mostly hidden from people who are devoted
to a lifestyle of selflessness and Christ-likeness.
This is a book that Satan dreads for you to read. The Enemy
Within is light to those who are in the darkness of despair. It's medicine for the loving or wounded hearts. A trusted safety road map for all who have been ensnared
in the jungle of wickedness. This is a book that

everyone will one day read, better now than later.
Dr Bernard Blessing
Rescue Life International

Table of Contents

Acknowledgements	5
Dedication	7
Introduction	8
Chapter 1: The Enemy Within	12
Chapter 2: Wounded in the House of "Friends"	21
Chapter 3: Household Enemies	25
Chapter 4: The First Murder Case!	32
Chapter 5: The Great Betrayal	35
Chapter 6: Absalom's Treachery	42
Chapter 7: Samson and Delilah	47
Chapter 8: Lessons of Life	57
Chapter 9: Faulty Foundations	61
Chapter 10: The Unholy Alliance	70
Chapter 11: Spiritual Ladder	83
Chapter 12: No More Hiding Place	92
Chapter 13: The Weapon of Prayer	100
Chapter 14: Gifts of the Holy Spirit	105

Chapter 15: The Wisdom Factor   111

Chapter 16: A Word to the Church!   116

Appendices   125

Acknowledgements

There are a few things in life that equal the blessing of being surrounded graced and gifted by selfless people. I consider myself blessed and indebted to many faithful helpers who regularly spend several hours and resources to make the ministry and myself what it is at this present time. Most of them are unnamed and you probably will never meet them on this side of heaven. Yet, their influence, contributions and fingerprints can be clearly seen in this book.

There are a few, who I believe, deserve special mention here.

To all members of World Harvest Christian Centre (WHCC); you have brought out the best in me – Thank You! To Dr Babatunde and family, Sister Nike & family, Pastor Ladipo and Sister B, Pastor Tim & family, Segun and family – I am greatly indebted to you all for your love and care!

To Daddy & Mummy, Elder and Mrs J.O Babatunde – I would not have wished to have any other parents; your word of encouragement kept me going!

Deaconess D. James – you are a mother in Israel! Pastor Adegboyega Carew – for always being there! May your children reap the fruits of the uncommon seeds you sowed into my life!

To Joshua, Grace and Jeremiah – You are my joy; you guys are simply the best!

To Adeoti Joseph Olaiya; you are a loyal son! Dr Bernard Blessing; you are truly a friend indeed! May your head never lack oil.

To the Holy Spirit, thank you for helping, strengthening and sustaining me!

Dedication

This book is dedicated to the Church militant, particularly those who are standing strong in spite of all the attacks and the bombardments from the enemy of our souls!

INTRODUCTION

To be in the company of beloved friends and relatives can be a heartwarming experience, laced with thrilling moments of joy and laughter. In some cases, expectations of sharing moments together in mutual interests make a whole lot of difference. No wonder the Psalmist exclaimed excitedly, *'I rejoiced with those who said to me, "Let us go to the house of the LORD." ' (Psalm 122:1, NIV)*.

Conversely, when we are amongst beloved, there are moments that strike fear and dread in our hearts. The root causes of such moments have either been experienced or witnessed. At other times, we have either heard of such scenarios, or read about them. Some names come to mind easily.

And there was David. And Abel. And Samson. Three individuals who stand out in the Bible. Though they appear at different periods in the Old Testament, they nevertheless share one thing in common; they were struck by the treacherous stabs of betrayal. In fact, Abel and Samson lost their lives because of these stabs.

Great men. Glorious destinies cut short. The handiwork of those close to them; the enemy within.

How many have been victims of such attacks? How many unsuspecting victims are busy worrying about those they perceive as enemies outside, whereas the real enemies are so close by. In our places of work, Church, even at home (down to family members and spouses).

Of a truth, most times, the enemy is just a breath away.

The Bible asserts in **Ephesians 1:3** that we have been blessed in Heavenly places. Jesus, however, points out in **Luke 17:1** that offences are sure to come. This statement implies that there will be stumbling blocks that will threaten to stunt the promises of God upon our lives.

This brings us to another person who was struck by the same stab of betrayal. He not only saw it coming, He knew exactly how to deal with it. In fact, it was coming from one of his trusted men. It cost him his life eventually. But the story didn't end there. He rose on the third day, just as He had predicted.

Yes, Jesus Christ the Son of God, the author and finisher of our faith. He conquered the treachery and what followed would re-define the battle between the forces of Heaven and the agents of the devil.

Beloved, betrayal and treachery may hurt, but it can be identified and overcome; even before it strikes.

Jesus declares in **John 3:31**, 'The one who comes from above is above all.' He knew Judas would betray Him. But He also knew what would happen.

Beloved, no matter how gifted or anointed you are, enemies will still lurk in the shadows, waiting to strike you. Their ultimate objective is encapsulated in the three-pronged agenda of the devil (John 10:10); to kill, steal and destroy. In no particular order, their objective is clearly defined from the start.

"How can I overcome?" you might ask.

Hebrews 12:1, 2 describes Jesus as the author and finisher of our faith. He is the best role model ever on how to overcome the attacks of the enemy within.

You can do the same.

Unfortunately, many are still grappling with how to deal with it.

Before I reveal to you how to exercise persistent victory over the enemy, allow me to walk you through the peculiar situations and scenarios that will help you in identifying how to handle such attacks. Real people. Real situations.

First, I will first show you, through the Bible, different cases of betrayal and the persons involved. I will further draw your attention to some real-life stories to elaborate on the issue. Then I will reveal to you sound Biblical insights to drive the point home.

Yes, you will know exactly how to identify the enemy within and overcome their schemes. You will get a firm grasp of how to navigate the murky waters of their treachery.

Many have fallen because they were too naïve to realize that the enemy they feared was some distance away, was actually in close proximity with them.

This book equips you to overcome such attacks decisively and with power from above

CHAPTER 1

THE ENEMY WITHIN

Yea, mine own familiar friend in whom I trusted, which did eat of my bread hath lifted up his heel against me.

Psalm 41:9 (KJV)

I was born, raised up and spent most of my youth in the South-western region of the most populous black nation on the earth; Nigeria. My mother-tongue is the Yoruba language, which I not only speak fluently, but I studied up to secondary school level!

I have discovered, like many people, that there's something very special about our mother-tongue! There are certain messages best communicated and understood in our mother tongue! As far as I can remember, I have learnt and spoken the English language ever since I was about three years old!

By the Grace of God, this is my twelfth book – all written in English language.

However, there are some truths and sentiments that I will love to convey, better expressed in my mother tongue.

Translating them into English almost means having them watered down. For the purpose of this chapter, I will share a few Yoruba proverbs and their meanings.

I believe they will best convey and express my message in this book;

> *"Eyinkunle n iota wa, ileniasenigbe"*
> **Translation**: One's enemy is in one's backyard, the one to hurt one lives with one. -
> **Anonymous**
> **Meaning-It is someone that is one's friends or household that can hurt one.**
> *"Kokoroti on je efo, idiefoni o wa"* **Translation**:-
> The insect that eats the spinach is in the spinach. - **Anonymous**
> **Meaning: It is only someone that is close to you that can hurt you.**
> *"Ti ikuile o ba pa eni, tiita o le pa eni"*
> **Translation**: If the death at home does not kill, the one outside the home is powerless to do so.
>   - **Anonymous**
> **Meaning: It is only someone that is close to you, (who knows your secrets) that can let outsiders on the secrets.**
> *"Ojulafeni, Ore odenu"*
> **Translation**:-Friend to the face but not at heart.
>   - **Anonymous**
> **Meaning: Pretentious friends.**
>
> *"Awonti o fiejesinusugbon won tuitofunfun jade"*
> **Translation**:-They have blood in them but spit out white saliva.   - **Anonymous**

Meaning: They have evil thoughts towards one but pretend to be friends with same.

"Ajenifeni, Ekuteile" **Translation:** One that bites and blows on the wound, the house mouse.   **- Anonymous**
Meaning: One should be wary of adversaries who pose as friends. While the animal hurts one, it also soothes at the same time, so as to continue hurting same.

You might be wondering whether we are taking lessons in Yoruba adages. On the contrary, I am simply trying to convey my thoughts in a manner most appropriate!

The commonality amongst all the proverbs above is this; one's greatest or most deadly enemies are not those who are far off, but the very persons that lay close to your bosom!

Most often, such persons go unnoticed in their devious guise. This is because they pose as friends! They are called the "unfriendly friends".

THE SECRET WEAPON

Satan is the greatest deceiver! His modus – operandi is to operate as a friend; an angel of light! This is the greatest strength of the enemy of our souls; the Power of Deception! He comes in as our aid – an advocate, an ally! But he always wears a mask,

"And no wonder, for Satan himself masquerades as an angel of light. It is not surprising, then if his servants masquerades as servant of righteousness. Their end will be what their actions deserve.

2 Corinthians 11: 14-15 (NKJV)

The prince of darkness and his cohorts always pretend to work for the advancement of the kingdom of light. Yet, their actions are always shrouded in secrecy that they may strike with ease. Their persistent waves of attacks are strategically meant to weaken your defences; that you may eventually cave in. Once control is achieved, destruction is inevitable.

Jesus Christ affirms the three-pronged agenda of the devil in John 10:10; **kill** (your joy), **steal** (your glory), **destroy** (your destiny). *Emphasis mine.* Do not be deceived, the enemy is forever within, pursuing the very same agenda!

History is replete with several women and men who were traitors; posing as friends but deep inside, treachery lurked.

Some did it for love, money or politics. However, one common thread within all of these individuals is that they changed the course of history forever. Some sold out on their countries, comrades and even their own families!

Let's consider a few of these traitors!

1. **VIDKUN QUISLING** – Leaked Norwegian military strategies to Adolf Hitler, who successfully occupied Norway. As reward, Hitler appointed him Premier. After the German surrender in Norway, Quisling was tried and convicted for deaths of 1000 Jews, along other war crimes. He was executed in 1945.

2. **ALDRICH AMES** - Ames sold American secrets to the Soviets for money, compromising over 100 United States Military Operations in the process and earning about $4.6million dollars for his efforts. 10 Americans were executed because their covers were "blown". In time, he revealed the names of every US agent in operation against the USSR. His lavish lifestyle raised red flags for the CIA. He was eventually arrested and convicted to life in Prison. His wife, Rosario, was deported to South America.

3. **BRUTUS** – Julius Caesar, self-appointed dictator-for-life of the Roman Empire was assassinated by a group of senators who conspired to kill him with the help of his own nephew, Marcus Julius Brutus. The famous quote, "Et tu, Brutus" was

uttered by Caesar as he took in the depths of his betrayal by his own nephew. Brutus committed suicide after losing the second battle of Philippi in 42 BC.

4. **ROBERT HANSSEN** –In 1979, Hanssen became involved with the Federal Bureau of Investigation (FBI) Counter Intelligence Unit and this paved the way for some of the most treasonous acts in American history. In 1983 Hanseen transferred to the Soviet Espionage unit within the FBI. Using his vast knowledge of computers, wire tapping and electronic surveillance, he went on to sell lists of FBI double agents and other moles to KGB (Russian Intelligence) agents for large sums of money. The FBI was able to arrest him with the help of Mike Hauck, his own brother-in-law.

The enemy succeeds because of their ability to blend in, to camouflage their real intentions until they are ultimately exposed. The proximity they enjoy with the people around them provides them the leverage so desperately needed in order to strike with precision.
For many, they are just among us, waiting for the opportune moment.

Secret Agent Within

A man headed off to a costume party some years ago dressed up as the devil. He had on a full-length red leotard, complete with horns and a tail. On his way to the party, his car broke down on a country road.

The only light he could see came from a building across the field; a Church.

Delighted, he set off to knock on the door, forgetting how he was dressed. The only thing racing through his mind was the sure possibility of receiving help from the Christian folks. Yes, they would help him fix his car, or so he thought.

As soon as he stepped through the door of the Church, everyone panicked. They frantically rushed through the windows. Some took the back door.

However, only one person refused to budge; a little old lady who stood defiantly, leaning on her cane.

He looked at her, just as she stared back at him. She then pointed in the direction of her car with her cane and said, "Now listen devil, I may have been a member of this Church for fifty years, but I've been on your side all that time!"

Just as this old lady had been Satan's emissary for over fifty years in the Church (sad to say), his agents (his tools) are forever among us; often undetected. Of a truth, the enemy is within!

CHAPTER 2:

WOUNDED IN THE HOUSE OF "FRIENDS"

"And one shall say unto him what these wounds in thine hands? Then he shall answer, those with which I was wounded in the house of my friends."
                    Zechariah 13:6 (KJV)

"A friend loveth at all times, and a brother is born for adversity."
                    Proverbs 17:17   (KJV)

A true friend loves at all times, no matter the situation or circumstances! Real friends stick by you in times of trouble. They bring healing, love, acceptance, and understanding! You never betray those that you truly love.

Nothing hurts more than a wound from a friend! How do you handle the treachery of a close friend or confidant? When friends hurt or harm us, the burden is often too difficult or heavy to carry! Many people have been known not to ever recover from the wounds or betrayal of a "friend".

The psalmist seems to express the sentiments of someone, who had been betrayed by a close companion. He remarks:

For it was not an enemy that reproached me; then I could have borne it: neither was it that hated me that did magnify himself against me; then I would have hid myself from him. But it was thou, a man mine equal, my guide, and mine acquaintance. We took secret counsel together, and walked unto the house of God in company.

Psalm 55: 12-14

Note the description of the person who betrayed and wounded the psalmist.
It was definitely not a person that he considered as an enemy; he confessed that if it was a known enemy, he could have endured it. However, this person was his personal guide, a companion. The person was truly an acquaintance or close friend!

What is more, it was an individual with whom he once enjoyed sweet fellowship! Indeed it was a person with whom he thronged into the house of God! A friendship had been built over a period of time. Unknown to him, the objective of the friendship was to hurt him.

If there is a place we all expect loyalty and safety, it is from the house of God! The last place you think you will ever experience treachery is from the household of Faith! However, this was not the lot of the psalmist.

Job also seemed to have taken this bitter pill himself. He remarked; *"All my intimate friends detest me; those I love have turned against me* (Job 19:19) NIV.

One of the critical questions on the lips of many in the Church of Christ today is this; why are so many ministers being taken out of the ministry? Why is there a rise in the abuse of the "Doma" gifts? Could it be that Satan has escalated his warfare on those who are in the frontline ministry? Without doubt, I believe this to be absolutely true!

If he is doing this, I know he has simply been perpetuating his three-pronged agenda since he fell as the anointed cherub!

However, I also believe that our adversary has also enjoyed the partnership and patronage of the Church; particularly those closest to God's servants.

Many of God's servants (including their families), are bleeding and in danger of death because they have been wounded in the house of their friends! The people they have been called to serve are the ones often responsible for sending them out of the ministry! The very ones that Church leaders are prepared to lay down their lives for are the ones that deal a death blow on their leaders!

After having served the Lord in the ministry for at least twenty five years, I have been greatly blessed to have worked for (and with) some God-fearing and loyal people! However, some of my greatest, deepest and most enduring wounds have been in the hands of the people I most loved, cherished and served with my whole heart.
But, I have also known and experienced the healing balm of Jehovah Raphar!

Unfortunately, some wounds are very deep; to the point of death itself.

Chapter 3

Household Enemies

"And a man's enemies will be those of his own household"-

Matthew 10:36   (NKJV)

Destiny destroyers and wasters are never far from each one of us! In fact most of us live and dine with those whose primary assignment is to abort our God given destinies! Some of these persons are people who carried you in their wombs for nine months; others are siblings!

One of such scenarios was the life of Joseph!

HATED FOR HIS DREAMS

"Now Joseph had a dream, and he told it to his brothers, and they hated him even more. So he said to them, "Please hear this dream which I have dreamed.

There we were, binding sheaves in the field. Then behold my sheaf arose and also stood upright, and indeed your sheaves stood all around and bowed down to my sheaf."

And his brothers said to him, "Shall you indeed reign over us? Or shall you indeed have dominion over us?" So they hated him even more for his dreams and for his words.

Then he dreamed still another dream and told it to his brothers, and said, "Look I have dreamed another dream. And this time, the sun, the moon, and the eleven stars bowed down to me."

So he told it to his father and his brothers; and his father rebuked him and said to him, "What is this dream that you have dreamed? Shall your mother and I, and your brothers indeed come to bow down to the earth before you". And his brother envied him, but his father kept the matter in mind.

Genesis 37:5-11 (NKJV)

Did you notice the source of the hatred Joseph suffered? His dreams! His dreams here represent his destiny, future, and God-ordained assignment! Your dreams will always attract enemies from the most unlikely source; your household! As long as you are perceived as a non-achiever, you will have no problems! But endeavour to rise up like an eagle (which you are), contentions, oppositions and obstacles become the order of the day.

Perhaps, Joseph's undoing is the problem that most people face today; being unable to guard their lips! Many people in life often start an unnecessary war, because they could not shut their mouth when God gives them a glimpse of their destiny!

Joseph invited trouble when he shared what was supposed to be between him and God!

Nowhere do we find in the Holy– writ that Joseph was mandated by God to share his dreams with his siblings!

Beloved, it is not everything downloaded to you from the third heavens that you are supposed to share with people! Consider such revelations strictly confidential.

There were things that Paul the Great Apostle heard when he was caught up into the third heavens, which he declared forbidden to be shared with mortal men!

"And I know such a man – whether in the body or out of the body I do not know, God knows how he was caught up into paradise and heard inexpressible words, which it is not lawful for a man to utter."

2 Corinthians 12: 3-4 (NKJV)

Too many ministers of the gospel and successful businessmen and women have courted trouble with their best friend, ministerial and business associates. How? When they sincerely shared with them their dreams, visions and projections for their lives and organisations.

Not everyone shares the same passion with your dreams and aspirations. Sadly, many have discovered this truth but in a hard way. Joseph is one such example.

JOSEPH IN THE PIT

"And it came to pass, when Joseph was come unto his brethren, that they stripped Joseph out of his coat of many colours that was on him;

And they took him, and cast him into a pit: and the pit was empty, there was no water in it.

Did you notice who cast Joseph into the pit? It was his own brothers! The next thing after casting him into a pit was to begin celebration; they began to eat bread! I prophesy to you right now, that everyone that is celebrating your downfall will be shamefully disgraced in the mighty name of Jesus!

Back to Joseph- note how his brothers were intent on putting him out of the picture.

"And they sat down to eat bread and they lifted their eyes and looked, and behold, a company of Ishmaelites came from Gilead with their camels bearing spicery balm and myrrh, going to carry it down to Egypt. And Judah said to his brethren, what profit is it if we slay our brother, and conceal his blood? Come, and let us sell him to the Ishmaelites, and let not our hand be upon him, for he is our brother and our flesh. And his brethren were content. Then there passed by Midianites Merchantmen and they drew and lifted up Joseph out of

the pit, and sold Joseph to the Ishmaelites for twenty pieces of silver : and they brought Joseph into Egypt

Genesis 37: 25-28 (KJV)

Observe the level of wickedness typical of household enemies. First, Joseph was dumped in a pit. Next he was sold to unknown traders! This is the height of wickedness! That children of the same father could do this to their own brother shows you how desperately wicked the heart of man is.

Have you ever wondered what they thought would become of him after his sale? He could have been resold, made a slave for the rest of his life or even killed! This is what envy does! It is as strong and deadly as death itself!

Thank God for His guiding hands; the extremities of Man are His opportunities! After men do their worst, then you can see God at His best! Indeed God works through the frailties of men! So true is Paul's writing to the Romans;

"And we know that all things work together for good to those who love God and are called according to His purpose."

Romans 8:28 (NKJV)

Again, Joseph saw God using his brother's wickedness to fulfil his divine assignment, when he declared repeatedly at the purpose of his afflictions:

"But now, do not therefore be grieved or angry with yourself because you sold me here; for God sent me before you to preserve life

Gen 45:5 (NKJV)

"But as for you, you meant evil against me; but God meant it for good, in order to bring it about as it is this day, to save many people alive"

Gen 50:20 (NKJV)

I prophesy over you today, that every plot by anyone against you, to bring you down by destroying you or your dream will backfire in the name of Jesus!

Every demonic agenda by household wickedness or any enemy within to abort your destiny shall bring about your promotion in Jesus name!

PROPHETIC PRAYER POINTS

- Every power within my family, trying to abort my destiny be destroyed in Jesus name!
- Lord Jesus, pull me out from the pit that household wickedness has put me in!
- Every demonic voice speaking against me- shut up and be silenced in Jesus name!
- Lord, let your hand deliver me from every slave market that household enemies have sold me!
- Lord, deliver me from all troubles and afflictions that my mouth has put me in!
- Father, everything that the enemy meant to destroy me with, use it for my promotion!

- Every God-given dream of mine that has been caged, be released by fire in Jesus name!

CHAPTER FOUR

Cain and Abel – The First Murder Case!

How many lives have been silenced at the peak of their career? How many cases do we read in the passages of the newspapers that daily baffle the best brains in our intelligence service, ultimately traced to the door steps of a younger or elder brother? The origin of murder can actually be traced not to an outsider, but an enemy within – a blood brother.

Again, like in the case of Joseph, the source was the spirit of envy! Abel's offering was accepted by God while that of his brother, Cain, was rejected. The result was the first case of murder in the scriptures (Genesis 4:8).

James 1:14, 15 describe the stages that lead to sin. Cain was caught up in these stages and murder became inevitable.

From the above, before sin is committed, it is first pre-meditated.

Now Cain talked with Abel, his brother. And it came to pass, when they were in the field, that Cain rose up against Abel, his brother and killed him.

Genesis 4:8 (NKJV)

The murderous spirit of Cain is still very much alive today! It pervades many of our homes and Churches!

Do you know how many spirits of hatred have developed as a result of your gifts, offerings, tithes to the house of God or other charitable or humanitarian causes? Do you know many people who get upset because they felt you gave more than them or you far exceeded their expectations?

As a Pastor I have had to settle serious quarrels between couples, when the husband discovered how much the wife was giving to the work of God! This almost caused a massive rift in the marriage; but for the wisdom of God. Could this be the reason why many people like to follow the biblical injunction of not sounding the trumpet or not allowing their right hand know what their left hand is doing !

"Therefore, when you do a charitable deed, do not sound a trumpet before you as hypocrites do in the synagogues and in the streets, that they may have glory from men. Assuredly, I say to you, they have their reward. But when you do a charitable deed, do not let your left hand know what your right hand is doing "

Matthew 6:2-3 (NKJV)

Prophetic Prayer Points

- Every spirit of murder in my bloodline against me, be neutralised in the name of Jesus!
- I shall not die but live to declare the works of the Lord!
- Let my offerings speak against every plot of my enemies in the name of Jesus!
- Every arrow of envy shot against me, return back to the sender in the mighty name of Jesus!
- Every plot to cut my life short should backfire in the name of Jesus Christ!

CHAPTER 5

THE GREAT BETRAYAL

Even my own familiar friend in whom I trusted, who ate my bread has lifted up his heel against me.

Psalm 41:9 (NKJV)

"Then one of the twelve, called Judas Iscariot went to the chief priests and said, "What are you willing to give me if I deliver Him to you." And they counted out to him thirty pieces of silver. So from that time, he sought opportunity to betray Him.

Matthew 26:14 -16 (NKJV)

Most of us must have experienced one form of betrayal or the other. Some from a business or ministerial associate or colleague, others from a close relative or sibling. Yet, some others may have experienced or endured the gruesome pains of betrayal from your most loyal friend, your wife or husband. However, the greatest betrayal of all time took place in the Middle East; in a garden in the land of Israel over two thousand years ago. It was hatched by a supposed friend. He was also an associate, a disciple and treasurer of the team. His name, Judas Iscariot.

It is the greatest betrayal of all time, not only because the story has endured two millennia, but the singular act led to an innocent man's gruesome death on the cross of Calvary. This sacrifice providentially brought about the redemption of mankind.

Judas was called by Jesus (along with the other eleven men) to be His disciple after a whole night of prayers.

"And He went up on the mountain and called to Him those He himself wanted. And they came to Him. Then He appointed twelve that they might be with Him and that He might send them out to preach and to have power to heal sickness and to cast out demons. Simon to whom He gave the name peter, James the son of Zebedee and John the Boanerges that is " Sons of Thunder. Andrew, Phillip, Bartholomew, Matthew, Thomas, James the son of Alphaeus, Thaddaeus, Simon the Canaanite and Judas Iscariot who also betrayed Him. And they went into a House.

Mark 3: 13 -19 (NKJV)

Not only was Judas part of the eleven, he was given power to heal the sick, cast out demons and preach the gospel. Furthermore, he occupied perhaps the most strategic position in the team; he was the treasurer.

If it were in modern-day government, he would have been the Minister of Finance or the Chancellor in the

U.K. Perhaps the next most strategic position after that of the Prime Minister.

It must be said that Jesus must have reposed so much trust and confidence in Him to have been the person handling the purse.

"Then Mary took a pound of very costly oil of spikenard, anointed the feet of Jesus, and wiped His feet with her hair. And the house was filled with the fragrance of the oil.
But one of His disciples, Judas Iscariot, Simon's son, who would betray Him, said, ^{5} "Why was this fragrant oil not sold for three hundred denarii and given to the poor?" This he said, not that he cared for the poor, but because he was a thief, and had the money box; and he used to take what was put in it."

John 12:3-6 (NKJV)

The above passage gives us a glimpse of a number of things. First, it reveals Judas' position in the team. He was the one that had the money box.

Secondly, and perhaps more importantly, like Gehazi (the servant of Elisha), his heart was filled with greed. Rather than care for his Lord or the ministry, his heart was engrossed with filthy lucre.

The scripture describes him as a thief; he always helped himself with the money that belonged to the team or ministry. Look around us today, does it appear familiar? How many Ministers of State, particularly in many African countries, do the same. This is probably the greatest hindrance to development and progress in the African continent. I have often argued in many places over the years that my country of birth, Nigeria (like many other African states), have only one major problem; bad leadership originating from greed.

I am sure most people will not be shocked if we say that most politicians are corrupt worldwide. However, what might be a shock is the level of greed in the church today, particularly among the so called Pentecostals.

Like Judas, a lot of Christian leaders are greedy for gain. Their belly is their god. Is it therefore a coincidence that Judas betrayed his Lord because of money? Are there lessons for all of us today? I believe a lot.

"And while He was still speaking, behold Judas one of the twelve with a great multitude with sword and clubs came from the Chief Priest and elders of the people.

Now His betrayer had given them a sign saying "Whomever I kiss, he is the one seize Him." Immediately he went up to Jesus and said, "Greetings, Rabbi!" and kissed him. But Jesus said to him, "Friend, why have you come?" Then they came and laid hands on Jesus and took him.

Matthew 26: 47-50

There are a number of important issues that the Holy Spirit wants to bring to our attention from this passage.

First, and perhaps most critical, was the personality of the betrayer; Judas. He was one of the twelve. I personally believe that apart from Peter, James and John, he was probably the next in line. He belonged to the inner circle. The betrayer was an enemy within.

Furthermore, it took an insider to give Jesus away to his enemies; the Chief Priest and the elders of the people. I have often wondered why Judas had to give a sign of a kiss before Jesus was arrested. Could it be the way Jesus always dressed and carried himself just like any one of the twelve? Jesus represented meekness. This made it extremely difficult to distinguish him from the rest, except with a kiss from His follower.

I believe this should be a great lesson for many of my Hollywood star preachers who are often dressed in sensual and very expensive garments; a far cry from the meekness of Christ.

Perhaps the most heart-rending part for me, reading through the episode of the betrayal, is when Jesus referred to Judas as a friend.

"But Jesus said to him, friend why have you come?"

Matthew 26:50a

I wonder how Jesus would know that one of His intimate disciples (Judas) would betray him for money, yet still refer to him as a friend? Was that supposed to prick his conscience? Did He say that to show His unfailing love, in spite of man's failings? Whatever this meant, surely it should leave a lasting impression in our hearts today on how to treat those who betray and despitefully treat us.

Finally, it is worth mentioning that when the Bible declares that Judas kissed Him (Jesus), it indicates more than a causal greeting. In the original Greek tradition, Judas gave to Jesus the affectionate and fervent greeting of intimate friends. What an irony? On the one hand, he gave an affectionate greeting of intimate friend while in reality in his heart, he was selling his most loyal friend (the lover of his soul), for just thirty pieces of silver.

How many of us have been betrayed, wounded and stabbed by our closest associate and those for whom we will readily lay down our lives? How many of you today have been kissed by your most intimate friend and confidant and yet, with one hand thrust the sword into your heart.

May God deliver us from enemies within, who also camouflage to be friends.

CHAPTER 6

ABSALOM'S TREACHERY

Apart from Abraham (the founder of the Jewish nation), and Moses (their deliverer, prophet and Law giver), there's no other personality throughout the Old Testament corpus that stands out like David (the psalmist, accomplished warrior and Israel's ideal King!).

Not only is Christ's Kingly ancestry traced to him, but the reigns of all Israel's righteous kings are often measured against that of David. As a soldier, shepherd, and then king, David fought and won many battles. However, the most celebrated was fight with Goliath, the champion from Gath.

David Defeats Goliath

"And David said to Saul, Let no man's heart fail because of him; thy servant will go and fight with this Philistine."

And Saul said to David, "Thou art not able to go against this Philistine to fight with him for thou art but a youth and he a man of war from his youth."

And David said unto Saul, "Thy servant kept his father's sheep, and there came a lion, and a bear, and took a lamb out of the flock. And I went out after him, and smote him and delivered it out of his mouth; and when he arose against me, I caught it by its beard, and smote it, and slew it.

Thy servant slew both the lion and the bear: and this uncircumcised Philistine shall be as one of them, seeing he hath defiled the armies of the living God."

David said, "Moreover, the Lord that delivered me out of the paw of the lion, and out of the paw of the bear, He will deliver me out of the hand of this Philistine." And Saul said unto David, "God and the Lord be with thee."

I Samuel 17: 32 – 37   KJV

That David was exceptionally bold is something that no one will question! For a man to slay both lion and bear with his bare hands is not only almost impossible, but also uncommon! These were some of his incredible credentials before facing Goliath!

To face and defeat Goliath was in itself something of a tall order! For anyone of David's age to defeat someone of Goliath's stature, strength and experience must have been nothing other than a miracle.

Ironically, the very man who dared and killed such an imposing figure as Goliath would soon face an enemy not as imposing, but from whom he would flee; his own son!

DAVID FLEES FROM ABSALOM

In the light of King David's exploits, it is a bit surprising that David fled from his own son; Absalom! Let's read the account –

After four years, Absalom said to King David, "Sir, let me go to Hebron and keep a promise I made to the Lord."

While I was living in Geshur in Syria, I promised the Lord that if he would take me back to Jerusalem, I would worship him in Hebron." "Go in peace," the King said. So Absalom went to Hebron. But he sent messengers to all the tribes of Israel to say, "When you hear the sound of trumpets, shout: Absalom has become King of Hebron!" There were 200 men who, at Absalom's invitation, had come from Jerusalem with him; they knew nothing of the plot and all went in good faith. And as he was offering sacrifices, Absalom also sent to the town of Gilo for Ahithophel, also one of King David's advisors. The plot against the King gained strength and Absalom's followers grew in number.

A messenger reported to David, "The Israelites are pledging their loyalty to Absalom." So David said to all his officials who were with him in Jerusalem, "We must get away at once if we want to escape from Absalom! Hurry or else he will soon be here and defeat us and kill everyone in the city."

II Samuel 15:9-14

Not only did David flee for his life, his closest officials and family members also left with him! The question that occupies one's mind is; what could have made a man so bold as to confront and kill bear and lion (as well as Goliath), to flee from his own son. Very simple; I believe it was because this particular "enemy" was from within!

A household enemy! It was someone who knew the King in and out! Absalom must have known his Father like the back of his hand! He must have been very conversant with his father's secrets, strengths and also his weaknesses. It is far more difficult to wage war against an adversary from within.

Perhaps, what must have compounded David's problems was the betrayal of his closest companion and confidant – Ahithophel! This must have dealt a massive blow to David! The pain of treachery from a son, coupled with betrayal from one's own closest confidant would have almost been unbearable to the King.

Thus the only best option was to flee the city.

"Even my best friend, the one, I trusted most, the one who shared my food, has turned against me.

                Psalms 41: 9   (Good News Bible)

CHAPTER 7

SAMSON AND DELILAH

"And the Lord God said, it is not good that man should be alone; I will make a help meet for him.

Genesis 2:18   (KJV)

"For man did not come from woman, but woman from man; neither was man created for woman, but woman for man."

I Corinthians 11:8-9   (NIV)

"For man was not (created) from woman, but woman from man; neither was man created on account and for the benefit of man."

I Corinthians 11:8-9   (Amplified)

"His mouth is most sweet: Yea, he is altogether lovely. This is my beloved, and this is my friend, O daughters of Jerusalem."

Songs of Solomon 6:16   (KJV)

*"Do not be yoked together with unbelievers for what do righteousness and wickedness have in common? Or what fellowship can light have with darkness? What

harmony is there between Christ and Belial? What does a believer have in common with an unbeliever?

II Corinthians 6:14-15 (NIV)

Marriage was instituted by God for a number of reasons. Amongst them is procreation or fruitfulness. God brought the man and the woman together in order to perpetuate their kind. Therefore, it is only within the marriage bonds that children are expected to be born and raised!

"So God created man in his own image; in the image of God he created him; male and female He created them. Then God blessed them, and God said to them, be fruitful and multiply; fill the earth and subdue it, have dominion over the fish of the sea, over the bird of the air, and over every living thing that moves the earth.

Genesis 1: 27-28 (NKJV).

Secondly, Marriage was instituted for companionship. After God created Adam and put him in the Garden with all kinds of animals, He saw a great need in Adam; the need for someone to relate with and share his life. God therefore declared in the following scripture:

And the Lord God said "It is not good that man should be alone; I will make him a helper comparable to him.

Gen 2:18 (NKJV)

Furthermore, marriage was established for multiplied effort, power and resources. This implies uncommon power in synergy.

"How could one chase a thousand, And two put ten thousand to flight...?"

Deuteronomy 32:30a

(New American Standard Bible)

Marriage was also instituted by God for couples to complement each other. This is because each one brings a unique gifting, resources and strength into the relationship. For this reason, couples are never to compete but complement each other.

The above now bring us to the following points:

1. ***Marriage is a union between a man and a woman who are genuinely committed to each other in love.***
2. ***Marriage is a personal conviction by either party to be there for each other, through thick and thin.***
3. ***Marriage partners deal with matters as a team; that is TOGETHER. They avoid nurturing cracks that will lead to collapse of marriage, or expose them to harm. Marriage partners are meant to be people who stand by each other***

> *as a team to fight a common foe! Marriage partners should never be party to anything that will be injurious to the wellbeing of their spouse! They must never expose their mate's secrets, weaknesses or anything that will endanger their lives or wellbeing.*

The enemy seeks to destroy marriages. That is why married couples (both the husband and wife) should make their union a spiritually formidable one.
However, this can only happen when you have a partner who is in agreement with the other partner. Alas, some are unequally yoked!

MARRIED TO A FRIEND OR A FOE?

In an ideal marriage, one should be married to your best friend; your greatest cheerleader. However, some people have been unfortunate to have been married to a foe! Many great men have met their early demise because they were betrayed; sold out by their own spouse, often because of money!

Samson was one of such great men in the Bible who met his unfortunate end in the hands of his supposed wife; Delilah!

He was a man destined for greatness right from his mother's womb. Not only was his birth announced by an Angel before he was born, the manner of his life and destiny were set forth (well before he took his first breath).

Samson was not only a Nazirite. His destiny was to deliver Israel out of the menace of the Philistines. In other words, he was a Judge (Judges 13)

As a Nazirite, he was to abstain from wine or strong drink and anything unclean, and his hair (the secret to his prowess) was to remain uncut or unshaved.

Samson's judgeship consisted of single – handed victories over the Philistines. This disrupted their dominance over Israel for about twenty years. Samson was indeed a thorn in their flesh. As a result, they tried everything to get rid of him. The Philistines sought every conceivable means to terminate his life because he had become more than a handful to them. They found him too powerful until they located an "enemy" within – Delilah!

Perhaps the greatest mistake that Samson made also was to marry Delilah, a woman from the valley of Sorek, thereby breaking divine injunction to the Jews never to marry people of other nations because of the dangers they posed (Deuteronomy 7: 1-4).

Let's read the account of the treachery of Delilah!

"Afterward it happened that he loved a woman in the valley of Sorek, whose name was Delilah. And the Lords of the Philistines came up to her and said to her, "Entice

him, and find out where his great strength lies, and by what means we may over power him, that we may bind him to afflict him; and everyone of us will give you eleven hundred pieces of silver."

So Delilah said to Samson, "Please tell me where your great strength lies, and with what you may be bound to afflict you."

And Samson said to her, "If they bind me with seven fresh bowstrings, not yet dried, then I shall become weak, and be like any other man."

So the lords of the Philistines brought up to her, seven fresh bowstrings, not yet dried, and she bound him with them.

Now men were lying in wait, staying with her in the room. And she said to him, "The Philistines are upon you, Samson!" But he broke the bowstrings as a strand of yarn breaks when it touches fire. So the secret of his strength was not known. Then Delilah said to Samson, "Look, you have mocked me and told me what you may be bound with." So he said to her, "If they bind me secretly with new ropes that have never been used, then I shall become like any other man."

Therefore Delilah took new ropes and bound him with them, and said to him. "The Philistines are upon you, Samson!" And men were lying in wait, staying in the room. But he broke them off his arms like a thread. Delilah said to Samson, "Until now you have mocked me and told me lies. Tell me what you may be bound with." And he said to her, "If you weave the seven locks of my head into the web of the loom"-

So she wore it tightly with the batten of the loom, and said to him, "The Philistines are upon you, Samson!" But he awoke from his sleep, and pulled out the batten and the web from the loom.

Then she said to him, "How can you say, 'I love you', when your heart is not with me? You have mocked me three times, and not told me where your great strength lies."

And it came to pass, when she pestered him daily with her words and pressed him, so that his soul vexed to death, that he told her all his heart, and said to her, "No razor has ever come upon my head, for I am a Nazirite to God from my mother's womb. If I am shaven, then my strength will leave me, and I shall become weak, and be like any other man."

When Delilah saw that he had told her all his heart, she sent and called for the lords of the Philistines; saying "Come up once more for he has told me all his heart." So the lords of the Philistines came up to her and brought the money in their hand. Then she lulled him to sleep on her knees, and called for a man and had him shave off the seven locks of his head. Then she began to torment him, and his strength left him.

And she said, "The Philistines are upon you, Samson," So he awoke from his sleep, and said, "I will go out as before, at other times, and shake myself free!" But he did not know that the Lord had departed from him.

Then the Philistines took him and put out his eyes and brought him down to Gaza. They bound him with bronze fetters and he became a grinder in the prison.

Judges 16: 4-21 (NKJV)

At this stage, a number of observations can be discerned!

1. Here again, we see one of God's generals betrayed by an enemy within (his wife) for money; eleven hundred pieces of silver.
2. Samson revealed what was meant to be a guarded secret – the source of his great power! This again raises the age long question; should you always reveal everything about yourself to your spouse?
3. Thirdly, and perhaps sadly, the Bible declares that after luring Samson to sleep, she began to torment him! For a married partner to torment her husband leading to his eyes being taken out is very pathetic.

    Samson's destiny was cut short. Perhaps he would have lived a lot longer; achieved greater feats, and subdued more of God's enemies!

Any lessons for those of us living in the 21st Century, particularly Ministers of the Gospel? I believe a lot!

The enemy within will always keep inquiring about confidential and private information in order to ascertain potential weak spots.

Let him that hath ears, hear what the spirit is saying.

CHAPTER 8

LESSONS OF LIFE

The chronicles of events inform us of the past that we may navigate with caution, the affairs of life and learn from any errors made. True life stories, in their own unique way, drive home a salient point; TREAD WITH WISDOM, OPERATE IN FAITH.

I will share with you two true life stories. Observe how the stories unfold and decipher the messages therein;

Girl Blinded by Mother

A certain minister of the Gospel who I know personally once had two visitors; a young girl accompanied by her mother. The minister was well experienced and popular for his gift in the ministry of deliverance. They had approached him for a solution to the girl's blindness. After listening to what both parties had to say, he directed them to a room where they would pray a prayer of agreement. The prayer was a declaration that the girl's blindness should go back to whoever it came from.

The prayers commenced and escalated in fervency. After a while, the girl screamed, "I can see!" At exactly the same moment, the mother became blind.

As shocking as the story may seem, such scenarios still occur. We must not forget that we live in a world ruled by the god of this age, who has blinded the eyes of those that are perishing (II Corinthians 4:3,4), thereby causing their conscience to be seared (I Timothy 4:2).

Pastors and ministers of the Gospel particularly need to consistently pray for the spirit of discernment. It is only through this gift that the deliverance minister could have discerned the mother as the source of the daughter's blindness. The enemy is not always as far as we have been made to believe. Most times, the deadliest of enemies are those close by.

Rose Displaces Angela

This story occurred in Ghana, in the city of Kumasi. Rose and Angela (not real names), had been best of friends for over thirty years. In fact, the friendship started in their childhood days. They eventually got married to their respective husbands.

Unfortunately, the husband to Rose, Shadrach, died in a ghastly car accident.

In such moment of grief and bereavement, what would you expect from Angela? "Comfort her friend and give her the needed support" you might say. Well, that was exactly what happened. Angela would often bring Rose to her home. Together with her husband, Daniel, they would counsel Rose, encouraging her and praying for her. It was common for Rose to spend weekends at their home.

This was where the ugly twist set in.

Rose began to seduce Angela's husband, Daniel. Initially, he resisted but Rose persisted with her devious scheme. She eventually succeeded in snatching her best friend's husband.

It might shock you to know how many homes have been broken by such wicked acts of seduction and treachery.

Relationships serve as operating space for any enemy attack. Through this proximity in relationships, weak spots can easily be detected and taken advantage of. Angela got stung by the betrayal of her best friend, Rose. Angela was the enemy within.

CHAPTER 9

FAULTY FOUNDATIONS

"If the foundations are destroyed, what can the righteous do?

Psalm 11:3 (NKJV)

"He is like a man building a House, who dug deep and laid the foundation on the rock. And when the flood arose, the stream beat vehemently against that house, and could not shake it, for it was founded on the rock. But he who heard and did nothing is like a man who built a house on the earth without a foundation against which the stream beat vehemently, and immediately it fell. And the ruin of that house was great.

Luke 6:48-49   (NKJV)

There are fundamentally two kinds of foundations - the good and the bad, or the solid and the faulty!

What is a foundation?

It is a solid ground that structures are built upon! It is the part of a building that is usually not visible to the ordinary eyes!

Using the above definitions, we can discern the importance of spiritual foundations! Every individual born into this world has a spiritual foundation, just as every house has a foundation.

It is the invisible part of our lives! It is our starting point! It is the root from which our destinies are built! With this definition, you can see that none of us are without foundations, just as there are no trees without roots! Roots always determine the fruit that a tree bears; whether good or bad!

Our foundation is our origin! As every tree has an origin, so does every individual!

Did you know, for example, that different kinds of blood run through your veins? Did you know that you are part of a family tree, from both your fathers' and mothers' side?

Your foundation has a great deal to do with your destiny! Many people are oblivious of this fact – this is why they suffer dire consequences!

The Lord lamented in Hosea 4:6

"Therefore my people are destroyed for lack of knowledge."

The problem is not just about ignorance, even though this could be deadly, but often it is about rejecting knowledge that is readily available!

"Therefore my people have gone into captivity because they have no knowledge

         Isaiah 5:13a NKJV

Did you know that a righteous, godly foundation can affect ones destiny! Even so will a wicked, ungodly foundation have serious consequences on a person, unless they take the right steps!

YOUR MOST STRATEGIC ENEMY

Beloved, please note. I have decided to include this chapter for various reasons! First, often when we speak about the enemies or forces that are contending against our destiny, what readily comes to mind is Satan, Principalities, Powers, Rulers of darkness, Witches, Wizards and familiar spirits.

Secondly, even when we direct our search light homewards, most times our spiritual radar is pointed at satanic vessels that we can see around us, including (but not exclusive to) our marriage partners, business or ministerial associates, siblings, or extended family members!

What many of us overlook is our family tree foundations, which may be faulty! We may be ignoring the enemy that is within (albeit strategically positioned), in our foundation!

This is why the Psalmist raised a rhetorical question

"If the foundation be destroyed, what can the righteous do"

Psalm11:3 (KJV)

It's almost like asking the question," What can one do in and with a storey building that the building experts have declared has a faulty foundation." The answer is obvious.

"Our Fathers sinned and are no more and we bear their iniquities"

Lamentations 5:7 (ESV)

"You shall not make for yourself a carved image of any likeness of anything that is in heaven above, or that is in the earth beneath, or that is in the water under the earth. You shall not bow down to them nor serve them. For I, the Lord your God, I'm a jealous God, visiting the iniquity of the fathers upon the children to the third and fourth generations of those who hate me. But showing mercy to thousands, to those who love me and keep my commandments."

Exodus 20:4-6 (NIV)

What lessons are the above scriptures trying to convey to us? It appears to warn that there's a spiritual impact (for decisions made or actions taken), on successive generations! In other words, the actions of our forebears may perpetuate its evil impacts on their offspring's, even if they never met!

Just as the actions of our ancestors may be good and righteous, so also can they be ungodly and wicked!

Without controversy, I have witnessed grace, favour, anointing and spiritual mantles transferred from one godly or righteous generation to the next! Examples abound all around us today. They include the Hagins, Copelands, Grahams, Cerullos etc.

If the above is true, so also can wickedness and ungodliness (with its attendant consequences), be passed on to the coming generations!

Some who are reading this book now are suffering from consequences of a faulty foundation. Your parents or grandparents might have long been gone. But, like Jeremiah lamented, we bear the fruits of their iniquities.

SOME CAUSES OF FAULTY OR EVIL FOUNDATIONS

The following are lists of what can cause an evil or faulty foundation. Please note that this list is not exhaustive!

- **Family Curses:** Many families are living under a curse! This could have been placed on them by someone or self – inflicted e.g. Gehazi (II Kings 5:27)
- **Idolatry**: Families known to have worshipped local or family deities for generations.
- **Membership of Secret Societies**: Like the Lodge, Rosicrucian, etc. It is even known that many students in campuses located within universities and institutions of higher learning belong to them.
- **Polygamous Homes**: Where parents have had multiple partners or marriages.

- **Witchcraft:** Your ancestors or yourself may have dabbled into witchcraft
- **Ungodly Covenants:** Where our ancestors might have entered into demonic covenants with people, evil association or local deities
- **Divination, Star Gazers, Necromancy:** Where a family has been heavily involved with familiar spirits or their like.
- **Membership of Royal Families:** Most often, what occurs in royal families is more than what meets the eye! Except a royal family has been fully dedicated to Jesus Christ, most royal families are heavily involved in rituals, demonic practices and secret societies! There are principalities and powers that rule such royal families.
- **Sexual Perversion:** Where your family tree has been heavily involved in various forms of sexual perversion, like the household of David; incest, homosexuality, lesbianism, bisexuality, prostitution, etc.
- Ritual Killings
- Priests and Priestess of deity or local gods
- Families with foundation in Islam, Hinduism, Buddhism, Shintoism, and other false or demonic religions.
- When family homes and buildings have been dedicated to or by the occult, witchcraft, secret societies or herbalist (shaman) etc

CURES FOR FAULTY FOUNDATIONS

Since we have considered some of the causes of a faulty foundation, it is also pertinent for us to look at the cures or solution!

- **Salvation through Jesus Christ**- The primary way of escape through a faulty foundation is to accept Jesus Christ as Lord and Saviour! This would commence the rebuilding of a new foundation.
- **Repent from all your sins**- Make sure you genuinely repent of all the sins you have committed in ignorance, and that of your ancestors. Great Intercessors in the Bible did the same – Nehemiah, Moses etc
- **Renounce Membership of all secret and demonic societies and destroy all their altars, charms, clothing etc.** Gideon did the same! (Judges 6:25).

- **Restitution**- Where possible, make restitution. Jesus and John the Baptist preached about restitution.
- **Deliverance**- Go for thorough deliverance in a Church that believes and practices it. Don't get into spiritual pride, arrogance or profitless arguments, whether or not deliverance is necessary after salvation! After twenty-five years in ministry, I can tell you point- blank that deliverance is very helpful and you will often reap its fruits.
- **Warfare Prayers**: Get into warfare prayers, there's a difference between prayer or making

- petition to God and warfare prayers that deals with Satan and his agents.
- Ask the Holy Spirit to re-arrange your foundation and shine His light into your family.

PROPHETIC PRAYER POINTS

- I release myself from every inherited or foundational bondage in Jesus name!
- Lord, I release your axe into my foundation to destroy every evil root.
- I reverse every evil curse that is upon my family tree in the name of Jesus.
- I break myself loose from every demonic cycle in Jesus name!
- The strongman in my paths loose, you are displaced and disgraced in Jesus name!
- I invoke the blood of Jesus to wash me and my generations, from every demonic impurities of my ancestors.
- Lord I thank you for a new beginning in my Life, Family, Business and ministry!

CHAPTER 10

THE UNHOLY ALLIANCE:

SATAN, THE WORLD AND THE FLESH

That Christians are constantly involved in spiritual warfare is a scriptural given! In his writing to the Ephesians, Paul the erudite scholar from Tarsus makes this truth expressly clear –

"For we do not wrestle against flesh and blood, but against principalities, against power, against rulers of the darkness of this age, against spiritual hosts of wickedness in heavenly places."

Ephesians 6:12   (NKJV)

However what I believe a lot of Christians are ignorant about are the areas or levels of spiritual warfare!

For this study I will like to highlight the three areas of warfare against every believer!

HEAVENLY HOST OF WICKEDNESS: This comprises Satan, and all his hosts of wickedness (Eph 6: 10 – 20). The spiritual warfare and tactics deployed in this realm is targeted at Christian- witnessing and Ministry.

Too often, when we speak of spiritual warfare, most Christian teachings and literature focus only on this aspect - thereby neglecting the other areas!

THE WORLD: – The second area of spiritual warfare that confronts every believer is the World. This warfare is usually targeted against our thought patterns, lifestyle and behaviour.

James addresses this issue succinctly;

"Where do wars and fights come from among you? Do they not come from your desire for pleasure that war in your members? You lust and do not have. You murder and covet and cannot obtain; you fight and war yet you do not have because you do not ask.

You ask and do not receive, because you ask amiss, that you may spend it on your pleasures. Adulterers and adulteresses! Do you not know that friendship with the world is enmity with God? Whoever therefore wants to be a friend of the world makes himself an enemy of God.

(James 4 v 1-4 NKJV) see (John 15 v 18-21)

THE FLESH – Consider Rom 8:5-8. The flesh is the last area of spiritual warfare! This area is often overlooked; yet very strategic to Satan! If there is something that Satan needs more than anything to co-operate with him in order to bring down a believer, it is the flesh!

Our Lord had to overcome this area of warfare/ temptation when he fasted forty days, after which hunger pangs set in hard (Matthew 4:1-11; Mark 1:12, 13; Luke 4:1-3).

The Bible clearly states in Matthew 4:4, *"And the devil said to Him, 'If you are the son of God, command this stone to become bread.'"*

What was Satan appealing to? His flesh!

In this area, the flesh is always in warfare against the spirit, with regards to obedience, submission and discipline.

Let's consider Galatians 5: 16, 17;

"I say then; walk in the spirit, and you shall not fulfil the lust of the flesh. For the flesh lusts against the spirit and the spirit against the flesh, and these are contrary to one another, so that you do not do the things that you wish.

In James 1:14, the basis for temptation is the flesh; its desires and lusts. No flesh, no temptation! Flesh is the seal of "our evil desire". Desire leads to Sin. Sin leads to Death. In that particular order.

However, there is hope.

But if you are led by the spirit, you are not under the law. Now the works of the flesh are evident, which are adultery, fornication, uncleanness, lewdness, idolatry, sorcery, hatred, contentious, jealousies, outburst of wrath, selfish ambitions, dissensions, heresies, envy, murders, drunkenness, revelries and the like, of which I tell you beforehand, just as I also told you in the time past, that those who practice such things will not inherit the kingdom of God (Gal 5: 18-21).

One of Satan's most strategic allies is within! It was what made the first couple fall in the garden! David, the great army general, psalmist, the ideal king of Israel and the only man ever described as a man after God's own heart, succumbed to this deadly agent ; the flesh. He was supposed to be at the war front but rather stayed at home and yielded to the flesh, committing adultery and subsequently, murder!

How many great men and women have become bread crust, by yielding to this old foe called flesh! No wonder, even the greatest of all apostles realised who this enemy is;

"For I know that in me (that is, in my flesh) nothing good dwell; for to will is present with me, but how to perform what is good I do not find. For the good that I will to do, I do not do; but the evil I will not to do, it is no longer I who do it, but sin that dwells in me. For I delight in the Law of God according to the inward man.

But I see another law in my member, warring against the Law of my mind and bringing me into captivity to the law of sin which is in my members. O wretched man that I am! Who will deliver me from this body of death?

I thank God – through Jesus Christ our Lord! So then, with the mind I myself serve the law of God, but with the flesh the Law of sin.

Romans 7: 18-25

CHAPTER 11

CHURCH SPLITS

Church splits are as old as the Church itself!

One of the common features that have affected the phenomenal Church growth that we have witnessed in the 21st century has been Church splits. However, what many Christians (and indeed Church leaders) are unaware of is that Church splits first occurred in Heaven before it was transported and manifested on earth!

CHURCH SPLIT IN HEAVEN

"How you are fallen from heaven, o Lucifer, Son of the morning"

How you are cut down to the ground, you who weakened the nations.

For you have said in your heart...

I will ascend into heaven,

I will exalt my throne above the stars of God;

I will also sit on the mount of the congregation on the farthest sides of the North;

I will ascend above the heights of the clouds,

I will be like the most high.

Isa 14:12-14   (NKJV).

In the above scripture, Prophet Isaiah gives some insight into how Lucifer fell from glory and was cast out of Heaven for pride and insubordination.

In the same vein, Prophet Ezekiel describes the splendour and glory of Lucifer in Heaven, prior to his fall, and the judgement that came with it.

Moreover the word of the Lord came to me saying son of man, "Take on a lamentation for the King of Tyre, and say to him, 'Thus says the Lord God:

You were the seal of perfection, full of wisdom and perfect beauty.

You were in Eden, the garden of God; every precious stone was your covering. The Sardius, Topaz, and Diamond, Beryl, Onyx and Jasper, Sapphire, Turquoise, and Emerald with Gold. The workmanship of your timbers and pipes was prepared for you on the day you were created.

You are the anointed cherub who covers. I establish you. You were on the holy mountain of God; You walked back and forth in the mist of fiery stones.

You were perfect in your ways from the day you were created; till iniquity was found in you.

By the abundance of your trading, you became filled with violence within, and you sinned; therefore I cast you as a profane thing out of the mountain of God; and I destroyed you, O covering Cherub, from the mist of the fiery stones. Your heart was lifted up because of your beauty; you corrupted your wisdom for the sake of your splendour;

I cast you to the ground,

I laid you before kings,

That they might gaze at you.

You defiled your sanctuaries

By the multitudes of your iniquities

By the iniquity of your trading,

Therefore I brought fire from your midst;

It devoured you,

And I turned you to ashes upon the earth

In the sight of all who saw you

                Ezekiel 28: 11-18   (NKJV)

The book of Revelations further gives a graphic account of the war that ensued in Heaven which led to the banishment of Lucifer and his cohorts from Heaven;

"And war broke out in heaven! Michael and his angels fought with the dragon; and the dragon and his angels fought, but they did not prevail, nor was a place found for them in heaven any longer. So the great dragon was cast out, that serpent of old, called the Devil and Satan, who deceived the whole world; he was cast to the earth, and his angels were cast out with him.

Revelation 12:7-9   (NKJV)

The above passages highlight the sin, rebellion and the eventual judgement meted out to this highly influential angelic being called Lucifer! The reference to him as the *"son of the morning"*, "*the anointed Cherub that covereth*", clearly demonstrate his placement in Heaven's hierarchy.

His basic sin was that of unchecked personal ambition; desiring to be equal to or above God! Is this not what happens, most times in cases of Church splits?

Often, the associate Pastor is not satisfied with his position as an assistant or a leader in whatever capacity he has been assigned to function. He tries to manipulate his way through, in order to dethrone the rightful person!

Furthermore, in Revelation 12, we see Lucifer lead one third of the "stars of heaven" or the angelic beings away in rebellion!

"And another sign appeared in Heaven. Behold, a great fiery red dragon having seven heads and ten horns, and seven diadems on his heads.

His tail drew a third of the stars of heaven and threw them to the earth. And the dragon stood before the woman who was ready to give birth, to devour her child as soon as it was born!"

               Revelation 12:3-4   (NKJV)

We must note that all the angels that Lucifer led away in rebellion against God were once faithful and loyal to God!

I have often remarked on this fact; Lucifer was able to persuade one-third of the angelic host in Heaven to rebel against God, their Creator. This means he was very influential in Heaven. No right thinking believer must ever under estimate Satan!

Herein lies the origin of Church splits! If Satan can succeed in breaking the congregation of the angels headed by God, then we wonder whether any Church here on earth can be immune from this cancerous disease!

A Personal Experience

I have been part of a Church split very early on in my Christian experience! Looking back now almost twenty five years later, I will fervently counsel any would- be leader to avoid such line of action like a plague!

As a young person, about proceeding to the university, I had joined a missionary-oriented ministry! I must confess, I couldn't have had a much better Christian foundation! My Pastor then was not only a true pastor at heart, but he was highly graced by God to raise, train and release emerging leaders!

He was not the founder of the ministry though. He was someone you will call a loyal son to the overseer! Our Church was like the model parish in the organisation. A lot of responsibilities laid on the shoulder of our Pastor (similar to that of Timothy to the Chuch at Lystra and Iconium or Titus to the new Church in Crete).

What came as a shock to many of us was when our resident Pastor suddenly told us that we were moving to a new site, with a new vision and a new name! The rest is history!

A few points are worth noting from this unique experience!

First, the very person the founder entrusted his Church unto his hands (a loyal son) was the one who took at least ninety percent of the members of the original

Church! Secondly, it is worth pointing out that my Pastor did not leave the ministry with the blessing of the founder; a thing that I have come to realise had serious spiritual repercussions!

Not long after the Church took off and made serious spiritual waves, did the glory began to wane! Twenty five years on, I am not sure the Church and the minister have recovered from this experience!

Go into Church history. Look at Church splits. You will find out that the personalities that had been prominent or leaders of the new Church or movement were people who had been very close to the set man or were at the helm of power!

CHAPTER 11

SPIRITUAL LADDER

" Hereafter, I will not talk much with you for the prince of this world cometh, and hath nothing in me."
John 14:30 (KJV)

" I will not speak with you much longer for the prince of this world is coming. He has no hold on me."
John 14:30 (NIV)

" I will not talk much with you more, for the Prince (evil genius, ruler) of the world is coming. He has no claim on me – he has nothing in common with me, there is nothing in me that belongs to him, he has no power over me.

John 14:30 (Amplified)

" Be sober, be vigilant, because your adversary the devil as a roaring lion, walketh about, seeking whom he may devour.

"Resist him, steadfast in the faith, knowing that the same afflictions are accomplished in your brethren that are in the world."

1 Peter 5:8 – 9 (KJV)

"In your struggle against Sin, you have not yet resisted to the point of shedding your blood."

Hebrews 12:4 (KJV)

"Ye have not resisted unto blood, striving against Sin".

Hebrews 12:4   (American Standard Version)

"You have not yet struggled and fought agonisingly against sin not have you yet resisted and withstood to the point of pouring out your own blood".

Hebrews 12:4 (Amplified)

"Wherefore let him that thinketh he standeth take heed lest he fall."

1 Corinthians 10:12   (KJV)

In the previous chapter, we identified that Christians are constantly engaged in a spiritual warfare. We further listed three fundamental areas of warfare that each believer must confront in order to overcome Satan. They are the Heavenly Hosts of Wickedness, the world System and the Flesh! Out of all these three, it seems the last one is the most overlooked and yet very strategic and deadly!

Some time ago, I was studying John 14:30. It was Jesus' statement shortly before He went to the Cross. The Lord spoke to me through it, on how Satan would always look for a spiritual ladder for the purpose of an alliance, as a means of defeating us. Usually, an alliance with our flesh.

Jesus declared, *"...for the prince of this world cometh and hath nothing in me."*

The NIV states it thus, *"...he has no hold on me."*

The Amplified version says, *"I will not talk with you much more, for the prince (evil genius, ruler) of the world is coming . And he has no claim on me. He has nothing in common with me, there is nothing in me that belongs to him, he has no power over me."*

Something happened to me close to four decades ago. I was very young in secondary school back then. One of my close friends lost some money in class. This money, if I can recollect, was meant to be paid for his termly school meals. Somehow, the money got missing. The usual thing was to bring this to the notice of the class. After the rounds of announcements and pleadings in the class, he finally brought it to the attention of our class teacher. In those days, we were terrified of our class teachers. These were the days when they were allowed to freely use the cane. After many enquiries, no one still confessed to taking the money. The class teacher then resorted to searching everyone's bag! I remember how confident I was simply because I had not stolen the money. I didn't have anything that belonged to my friend, which could lead to trouble.

Conversely, I vividly remember when I was in Primary Three. I would help manage my mother's provision store. While at work, it was customary for me to help myself with some money made from sales. This continued for months, undetected.

Unfortunately for me, I was caught one fateful day. Not by my mother, but by a classmate who had requested that I buy him some ice cream. He had somewhat noticed that I always had money on me. I turned down his request for ice cream. He then queried me on how I had so much money on me. Since I had no reasonable explanation, he reported me to the class teacher. The class teacher cross-examined me and found out that I had helped myself, just like Judas.

A schoolmate was instructed to take me home and report me to my parents. The journey from my school back home usually should take about twenty minutes. However, on this day in particular, it took me almost an hour. This was my longest journey home. I was more petrified not of my mother's reaction but my fathers, because he was a professional at beating as a punitive measure.

What was my sin? I was caught with money that didn't belong to me. Hence, I had to suffer the consequences. When Jesus declared that the prince of this world was coming and he hath nothing on Him (or "he has no hold on him"), what was He saying? Very simple, there is nothing evil or shady, no unrighteousness in my life. I don't have any besetting sins that can give Satan a foothold in my life. Friend, Satan's modus operandi is always to look for a spiritual ladder through which he can climb to gain an entrance or take an advantage over us.

Sometimes it is a besetting sin like greed which was the ladder that Satan used to get Judas to betray His master. The same was true for Gehazi, who inherited leprosy rather than a double or triple portion of the anointing.

Sometimes the ladders that Satan will use are people especially those closet to us. If Satan wants to attack a righteous or godly person, and he finds no entry point, he can use family members or a very close associate.

What was the entry point or spiritual ladder for truncating Samson's ministry'? None other than the wife; DELILAH!

Furthermore, in order to trace the present crisis between the Arabs and the Jews, observe how our father in the faith raised children from Hagar. It took someone within (Sarah) to put pressure on him. He yielded to this temptation. It is not only vital for us to examine ourselves always to see whether there's any evil way before us, but it is also very essential that we pray constantly for deliverance from any snare and powers of darkness.

We should forever take the wise counsel of Paul the Apostle, when he declared;

Wherefore let him that thinketh, he standeth take heed lest he fall

I Corinthians 10 :12 (KJV)

PRACTICAL STEPS TOWARDS DEALING WITH SPIRITUAL LADDER

1. **Repentance:** If you struggle with a besetting sin, quickly get rid of it by genuine repentance. Nothing breaks the back of Satan more than repentance. As long as you live in darkness, you are a candidate for Satan's onslaught.

2. **Accountability:** I strongly believe in accountability. The bible teaches it. Not only are we all accountable to God and the brotherhood for the way we conduct ourselves, but we must also look for people who love us enough to confront us in love when we err. Every King David needs a Prophet Nathan who can confront you and declare you are the man.

3. **Watchfulness:** The Bible not only teaches us that we must constantly pray but we are to be watchful. Let's consider a few passages:

"Take ye heed, watch and pray, for ye know not when the time is"

Mark 13:33 (KJV)

"Therefore let us not sleep, as do others but let us watch and be sober"

1 Thess. 5:6 (KJV)

"But the end of all things is at hand be ye therefore sober and watch unto prayer.

1 Peter 4:7 (KJV)

4. **Guard Your Mouth**: Many people today have been snared by the words of their mouths. The enemy within has taken advantage of our unbridled tongue. What was the undoing of Joseph and Samson? It was not being able to keep secrets. There are certain secrets that should remain between us and God. I believe Joseph did not have to share his dreams with his envious brothers. Neither should Samson have succumbed to the pressures of dangerous and damming Delilah.

Build your spirit and integrity through the Word of God that the enemy may perceive you as being spiritually formidable. Follow the above steps and watch your spiritual walk with Christ grow from strength to strength.

CHAPTER 12

NO MORE HIDING PLACE

"And when Paul had gathered a bundle of sticks, and laid them on the fire, there came a viper out of the heat, and fastened on his hand. And when the barbarians saw the venomous beast hang on his hand, they said among themselves, No doubt this man is a murderer, whom, though he hath escaped the sea, yet vengeance suffereth not to live. And he shook off the beast into the fire, and felt no harm."

Acts 28:3-5   (KJV)

In this chapter, I will like to share with you one of the key ways to defeat an enemy within! This is both applicable to an individual, as well as the corporate body of Christ!

Satan is a master strategist! He operates with wiles and schemes. He often masquerades himself in order that the undiscerning never discover his plots.

In Genesis 3, he is introduced as a serpent. I think there is a reason why the scripture introduces him as a serpent and not a dog or an elephant.

Notice how the Holy writ describes him.
"Now the serpent was more subtil than any beast of the field which the Lord God had made". (Gen. 3:1) KJV.
"...Now the snake was wiser..." (Bas)

"...the shrewdest..."(Tor)
"...the wisest of all the beasts..." (Sept)
"...the most clever of all the wild beasts..." (AAT)

"Of all the beast the Lord God had made, there was none that could match the serpent in cunning". (Knox)

Throughout the scriptures we see that Satan appears or manifests himself in different forms through different means and vessels, depending on what needed to be accomplished!

In Acts 28, Paul encounters this same snake that brought about the downfall of the human race. He had, at different occasions, encountered this same snake in different cities and nations during his missionary journeys!

This viper, as is characteristic of snakes, would have been hiding somewhere, waiting for an opportune moment to strike at its prey!

However, we are told that Paul gathered some sticks and laid them on the fire. Unknown to him, a viper surfaced as a result of the heat!

Did you get that?

I hope you did not miss what the Holy Spirit is trying to reveal to you. It was the fire rekindled by Paul that exposed the viper; the result of the heat. Did you know that someone might have lost their life as a result of an attack that might have ensued?

In the case of Apostle Paul, he was immune to the effects of the attack. He simply shrugged off the viper.

In Africa, where I was raised as a boy, we have some of the most dangerous snakes known to man. Bush fires are also a common phenomenon in many parts of the continent. It is a common sight to see dangerous animals, including snakes, flee when bushes are set on fire.

In the same vein, Satan cannot withstand the heat that is generated from intense prayers! Witches, wizards and rascals from the satanic kingdom cannot remain unexposed for long where there is serious heat from our prayers.

THE NEED OF THE HOUR

If there is something that we need so fervently this present time, it is strategic and high level prayer power. The curse of this hour is a prayer-less church. Needed urgently in this critical hour are prayers.

The Pastor who is not praying is playing. The people who are not praying are straying. The church is today into many things, but is most stricken here; in the place of prayer. We have many organisers but few agonizers (who travail on their knees), many players and payers, few prayers. Many singers, few clingers. Lots of pastors, few wrestlers. Many fears, few tears. Many interferers, few intercessors.

Failing here, we fail everywhere.

(Leonard Ravenhill, Why Revival Tarries, Bethany House; 1992 version, Sovereign World, Ton Bridge)

What the Holy Book declared over two thousand years ago is still very true today in the 21st century.

" The effectual fervent prayers of a righteous man availeth much. "

(James 5:16b, KJV)

"The supplication of a righteous man availeth much in it's working."

(James 5:16b, ASB)

"Powerful is the heartfelt supplication of a righteous man."

(James 5:16b, Weymouth)

"The prayers of the righteous have a powerful effect"

(James 5:16b, Moffat)

"Tremendous power is made available through a good man's earnest prayer."

(James 5:16b, Phillips)

"Great is the power of a good man's fervent prayer"

(James 5:16, TCNI)

"The prayer of a righteous man has great power in it's effect." (James 5:16b, RSV)

"When a just man prays fervently there is great virtue in his prayer."

(James 5:16, KNOX)

"An upright man's prayer, when it keeps at work is very powerful."

(James 5:16b, WMS)

"The prayer of a righteous man can bring powerful results."

(James 5:16b, Norlie)

The earnest (heartfelt, continued) prayer of a righteous man makes tremendous power available [dynamic in its working].

(James 5:16b, Ampliified)

This is the kind of prayer that we need at this dark hour - dynamic, persistent agonising, effective prayers that obtain results!

WHY COULD THE VIPER NOT HARM PAUL?

The natives in Malta were greatly perplexed after they observed the snake fastened on Paul's hand yet not able to harm him! Their perplexed looks were no different on initially thinking the same Paul as being murderer at first, but now perceiving him as a god.

"I have said, ye are gods' and all of you are the children of the most high"

Psalm 82:6 (KJV)

What was responsible for Paul being unharmed by a deadly snake? The only answer I can think of was that Paul had been immunised through prayer power! It was impossible for the viper to have taken Paul out. First, he was the chief of all apostles, a man given to prayers. Secondly, he was constantly being sustained (kept alive) by the prayers of the saints, (the churches he had oversight over). Notice also that it was impossible for the viper to harm a "god".

When the temperature of our prayers is greatly increased, we will not only neutralise the spiritual toxins and venoms that our old adversary releases against us, but he will become exposed and then we can deal with him decisively and squarely!

TIME TO UNLEASH FIRE!

" For our God is a consuming fire."

Hebrews 12:29   (KJV)

There are different ways that God is portrayed or manifested in the Bible. One of such manifestations is as fire.

In Acts chapter 2, we see God manifesting on the early disciples in the upper room in the form of fire.

And there appeared unto them cloven

tongues like as of fire .

Acts 2:3   (KJV)

Again, at the call and commissioning of Moses, God appeared to him in the burning bush (Exodus 3:1-2). The writer of Hebrews further declared that our God is a consuming fire! This means HIS presence not only exposes darkness, but also destroys the works and agents of Satan. Any spiritually matured believer can attest to this fact; **even though God is sovereign and All-Powerful, He can do little or nothing, except we invite him through our prayers**.

What we therefore do when we refuse to pray is that we tie the hands of the Omnipotent One, thereby giving permission to the snake to go on rampage. Conversely, when we pray, we release God's fire. God is a consuming fire. When we pray fervently, we release fire which ultimately destroys and exposes the enemy of our soul.

Beloved, it is time to pray, it is time to travail. Indeed, it is time to expose the viper for there are no more places for hiding, no darker crevices from where to strike.

CHAPTER 13

THE WEAPON OF PRAYER

Pray without ceasing.

1 Thessalonians 5:17

And when He came to the place, He said to them, "Pray that you may not enter into temptation."

Luke 22:40

English Standard Version

Then He said to them, "Why do you sleep? Rise and pray lest you enter into temptation.

Luke 22:46 (NKJV)

For we do not wrestle against flesh and blood, but against principalities, against powers, against the rulers of the darkness of this age,[a] against spiritual hosts of wickedness in the heavenly places.

Ephesians 6:12 (NKJV)

Praying always with all prayer and supplication in the Spirit, being watchful to this end with all perseverance and supplication for all the saints—

Ephesians 6:18 (NKJV)

Then He spoke a parable to them, that men always ought to pray and not lose heart.

Luke 18:1 (NKJV)

What is Prayer?

Prayer can be described as earth's beckoning for Heaven's reckoning!

Prayer is pouring out our soul to God!

Prayer can also be seen as the channel through which Heavens' invisible resources can be released to mankind!

Prayer, in its simplest definition, is communion or communication with God!

However, we will also be right to see prayer as a weapon; albeit invisible, but the most potent weapon known to man!

According to Paul the Apostle, Christians are waging an invisible war with an invisible host of wicked spirits who are not only bent on frustrating every effort of kingdom advancement, but they are out to abort people's destinies!

In order to wage a good warfare, God has equipped believers with superior armoury; weapons to stop and defeat all the intrigues, manipulation, schemes and onslaught of the devil and his cohorts.

As Satan's time gets increasingly shorter by the day, so does his rage, fury and attacks become increasingly fierce, and lethal!

Therefore rejoice O heavens, and you who dwell in them! Woe to the inhabitants of the earth and the sea! For the devil has come down to you, having great wrath, because he knows that he has a short time."

Revelation 12:12 (NKJV)

In order to defeat Satan and his cohorts (who sometimes employ the services of the likes of Jezebel, Delilah, Cain and Judas), we must be regularly involved in warfare prayers!

Since prayer is as powerful or potent as God, then the believer can be rest assured that he can defeat or overcome intrigues from any enemy of his soul, including the unfriendly friends.

As Christians, we are charged to pray without ceasing (I Thessalonians 5:17). To be victorious in these evil days. Christians must watch and pray because our adversary is busy roaming around seeking whom he may devour.

Be sober, be vigilant: because your adversary the devil walks about like a roaring lion, seeking whom he may devour.

1 Peter 5:8 (NKJV)

FIGHTING A GOOD FIGHT

So let's not get tired of doing what is good. At just the right time we will reap a harvest of blessing if we don't give up.

Galatians 6:9 (New Living Translation)

Jesus told his disciples, "Situations that cause people to lose their faith are certain to arise.

Luke 17:1 (GOD'S WORD® Translation)

All praise to God, the Father of our Lord Jesus Christ, who has blessed us with every spiritual blessing in the heavenly realms because we are united with Christ.

Ephesians 1: 3 (New Living Translation)

Beloved, we have been equipped to advance the Kingdom of God on Earth. The devil will stop at nothing to ensure we do not fulfil the mandate of God upon our lives. This is why he uses our thoughts, our relationships and situations to rattle us to our very soul, in order to conform us to his devices.

Yes, the enemy may be within, but I John 4:4 authoritatively affirms and declares,

But you belong to God, my dear children. You have already won a victory over those people, because the Spirit who lives in you is greater than the spirit who lives in the world.

    1 John 4:4 New Living Translation

The Holy Spirit will comfort you in your time of need, to give you strength for battle, wisdom for trying times, and a renewed mind,

For God did not give us a spirit of timidity, but a spirit of power, of love and of self-discipline.

    II Timothy 1:7 New International Version

Never give up. Entertain no fears. Brace yourself. The enemy will never succeed in your life! Amen!!

CHAPTER 14

OPERATIONS OF THE GIFTS OF THE HOLY SPIRIT.

" There are diversities of gifts but the same Spirit. There are differences of ministries but the same Lord. And there are diversities of activities but it is the same God who works all in all. But the manifestation of the Spirit is given to each one for the profit of all. For to one is given the word of wisdom through the Spirit, to another the word of knowledge through the same Spirit.

> 1 Corinthians 12:4-8 (NKJV)

"To another the working of miracles, to another prophecy, to another discerning of spirits, to another different kinds of tongues, to another the interpretation of tongues.

> 1 Corinthians 12:10 (NKJV)

Having then gifts differing according to the grace that is given to us, let us use them. If prophecy, let us prophesy in proportion to our faith.

> Romans 12:6 (NKJV)

If there was a time that the church needed the operations of the gifts of the Holy Spirit more than ever (particularly the revelatory gifts), it is now. At this eleventh hour, we can no longer be spiritually naive.

We are reaching the closing days of the end times; when the wolves in sheep clothing are increasingly invading the church, when Satan and his agents are representing themselves as angels of light and ministers of righteousness.

We desperately need the manifestation of the gifts of the Holy Spirit, particularly the words of wisdom, knowledge, the gift of prophecy and the discerning of spirits.

Perhaps, it might be helpful to define some of these manifestations.

- **WORD OF KNOWLEDGE.** – The God-given ability to receive from the Holy Spirit (by revelation) the knowledge of facts and information which is humanly impossible to know.

- **PROPHESY** – there are at least 3 levels of prophecy.

1) **The Spirit of Prophesy** (Rev. 19:10) – When the Holy Spirit mantle of prophetic anointing enables a believer (or body of believers) to prophesy the word of the Lord. Without occasion of special endowment he would not normally prophesy. (

Source: The New Testament Church and Its ministries; Bill Scheidlea page 94)

2) **The Gift of Prophesy**: This is one of the nine gifts of the spirit and it operates under the same guidelines as any of the gifts of the spirit. The exercise of this gift is usually limited to edification, exhortation and comfort (I Cor. 14:3)

3) **The Ministry of the Prophet** (Eph. 4:11): This ministry is one of the DOMA or ascension gifts. People who operate in this ministry are regarded as one of the traditional offices of the New Testament. Unlike the person, with the gift of prophecy, the prophet is not limited to the realms of edification, exhortation and comfort. He may also operate in the realms of confirming, guidance, rebuke, warning, judgement and correction

   - **DISCERNING OF SPIRITS**: A gift that discerns the activities and manifestations of the spirits, whether good or evil, and the ability to deal with them.

What is common with all these gifts or manifestations is the ability to see beyond the natural.

How can we deal with the influx of prophets into the church today particularly those who come as wolves in sheep clothes? How can we spot the difference between sheep, goat and wolves?

How are we going to succeed in exposing those operating under the spirit of divination like the slave girl in Acts 16: 16-24?

Except we are full of the Holy Spirit and operate in these gifts.

How do we expose the hypocrisy of modern day Ananias and Sapphira?

Except by the operation of the Word of Knowledge?

(Acts 5:1-11)

How was Prophet Elisha able to expose Gehazi's greed, except by the revelation of the Holy Spirit. (II Kings 5:26)

If there is a time we need the Holy Spirit and His gifts to reveal the agenda, motives and scheming of God's enemies and ours too (those pretend to be friends), it is now.

Lord baptise us once again with the power of the Holy Ghost so that we may be helped to deal with all the enemies who are within the camp.

A People Equipped

But to each one of us grace has been given as Christ apportioned it. This is why it says:
"When he ascended on high, he led captives in his train and gave gifts to men."

> Ephesians 4:7, 8 (NIV)

A spiritual gift equips a believer to accomplish God's mandate upon his life, primarily to serve others. The gifts are diverse as listed in I Corinthians 12. They fall into three categories.
They are the
- POWER GIFTS- the gifts of healing, miracles, and faith;
- SPEAKING GIFTS- the gifts of prophecy, tongues, and word of knowledge;
- DISCERNMENT GIFTS- the gifts of word of wisdom, discernment of spirits, and interpretation of tongues.

Any Christian who seriously desires to serve God can pray to God for an impartation from the Holy Spirit. An impartation from the Holy Spirit can be a release of the gifts and/or power of God to move in the areas of ministry that motivate our hearts.

This in turn brings up the motivational gifts found in Romans 12. They fall into seven categories; **serving, teaching, exhortation, giving, prophecy, mercy,** and **leadership**.
(Source: Marc Dupont Ministries)

When Ephesians 1:3 declares that we have been endowed spiritually from the Heavens, I believe the gifts are part of our spiritual endowments.

They are for our use, to the glory of God, that the works of Satan will be defeated consistently, and for edifying the Body of Christ.

CHAPTER 15

THE WISDOM FACTOR

Wisdom is better than weapons of war...

Ecclesiastes 9:18a(NIV)

Wisdom is the principal thing; Therefore get wisdom. And in all your getting, get understanding.

Proverbs 4:7(KJV)

For wisdom is a defence as money is a defence. But the excellence of knowledge is that wisdom gives life to those who love it.

Ecclesiastes 7:12 (KJV)

And Jesus increased in wisdom and stature, and in favor with God and men.

Luke 2:52 (KJV)

How does one deal with a 21st century version of Judas' betrayal; a person who will sell out their most loyal friends because of money?

How will a modern day Joseph escape the arrows of envy fired from his own siblings, specifically meant to abort his dreams?

How on earth can a Nazarene Samson overcome the treachery and unholy alliance between a supposed "wife" who was bent on aligning with God's enemies to truncate the destiny of a deliverer?

I believe, without a shadow of doubt, that as the war between God's kingdom and that of Satan is getting to unparallel proportions, we will need the force of wisdom! While the agents and vessels of darkness are getting smarter, more cunning and more sophisticated, we the Sons of Light must begin to work in heavenly wisdom, which might have been unknown for several ages!

Look closely at the life of Jesus – our Saviour and model. Observe that His application of wisdom was a strong factor that made Him overcome all the schemes, trappings and snares of those who trailed Him right from the inception of His ministry. He knew when to speak and when to be quiet! He knew when His detractors wanted to entrap Him with His own words! He even knew exactly when to escape and when His life was in danger because He knew His time had not yet come!

I have often wondered why Jesus was so successful in His life and ministry, especially amongst several enemies, including those who pretended to be friends! If you study the scriptures carefully, observe how one of his keys to success was the fact that He never gave Himself to men; He knew what was in man!

Even when Judas betrayed Him, I believe His life was never taken; He simply laid it down,

He was oppressed and afflicted, yet he did not open his mouth; he was led like a lamb to the slaughter, and as a sheep before her shearers is silent, so he did not open his mouth.

Isaiah 53:7 (NIV)

Jesus knew, well before hand, all the evil intentions of Judas and He even alerted him (John 13:27).

What about the life of Samson – any lessons for us at all?

I believe several! However, the most important thing that Samson could be termed as being is foolish! I believe there are certain secrets that should be between a man and God alone! Should he have kept the secret of his strength to himself alone? Most likely he would have lived longer and achieved far more exploits for God!

Another lesson is that if he had read the books of the wise man Solomon (particularly Proverbs), he would have learnt about the dangers of getting attracted to and marrying strange women!

Again, like Samson, Joseph could have learnt from the wise sayings of King Solomon; there's a time to speak and a time to be silent (Ecclesiastes 3:7b). Had Joseph sealed his lips, he would have avoided the untold sufferings of 13 years! However, we do know that man's extremities are God's opportunities.

How did King Solomon administer justice between the two harlots who lived in the same house and were disputing on the ownership of the living child? The sheer force of wisdom. Let us consider the testimony and verdict of the scriptures on this matter –

And all Israel heard of the judgment which the king had rendered; and they feared the king, for they saw that the wisdom of God was in him to administer justice."

1Kings 3:28 (NKJV)

Without doubt, if there was something that we desperately need today to overcome the enemies within (particularly those that pretend to be friends), it is wisdom.

If any of you lacks wisdom, let him ask of God, who gives to all liberally and without reproach, and it will be given to him.

James 1: 5 (NKJV)

CHAPTER 16

A PROPHETIC WORD TO THE END TIME CHURCH

[7] "He, who has an ear, let him hear what the Spirit says to the Churches…" (Rev 2:7a)

[11] "He, who has an ear, let him hear what the Spirit says to the Churches…" (Rev 2:11a)

[17] "He, who has an ear, let him hear what the Spirit says to the Churches…" (Rev 2:17a)

[1] Now the serpent was more cunning than any beast of the field which the LORD God had made. And he said to the woman, "Has God indeed said, 'You shall not eat of every tree of the garden?,' "
[2] And the woman said to the serpent, "We may eat the fruit of the trees of the garden; [3] but of the fruit of the tree which is in the midst of the garden, God has said, 'You shall not eat it, nor shall you touch it, lest you die.'"
[4] Then the serpent said to the woman, "You will not surely die."
(Gen 3:1-4)

Many years ago, I read a book which I consider a prophetic classic. It depicts the spiritual warfare that the end-time Church will be confronting. The book is **The Final Quest** by Rick Joyner.

In this book, Rick Joyner describes the vision of the demonic army that Satan was deploying against the Church; their weapons and strategies. He writes:

"The demonic army was so large that it stretched as far as I could see. It was separated into divisions, with each carrying a different banner. The foremost division marched under the banners of Pride, Self-Righteousness, Respectability, Selfish Ambition, Unrighteous judgement and Jealousy. There were many more of these evil divisions beyond my scope of vision, but those in the vanguard of this terrible horde from hell seemed to be the most powerful. The leader of this army was the Accuser of the Brethren himself.

The weapons carried by this horde were named. The swords were named 'Intimidation', the spears were named 'Treachery', and the arrows were named 'Accusation, Gossip, Slander and Faultfinding'. Scouts and smaller companies of demons – with such names as 'Rejection; Bitterness; Impatience; Un-forgiveness and Lust' – were sent in advance of this army to prepare for the main attack."

On the strategy employed by Satan, Rick Joyner writes further,

" The primary strategy of this army was to cause division on every possible level of relationship; Churches with each other, congregations with their pastors, husbands and wives, children and parents, and even children with each other .

The scouts were sent to locate the openings in Churches; families or individuals that such spirits as 'rejection, bitterness and lust' could exploit and enlarge. Through these openings would pour demonic influences that completely overwhelm their victims. (RICK JOYNER; **The Vision**, THOMAS NELSON; NASHVILLE, 2000, pg 11-13)

On The Backs of Christians

What intrigued me most about the book was who Satan was using to accomplish his mission or wage his battle!

Rick Joyner continues: - *"The most shocking thing about this vision was that this horde was not riding on horses but permanently on Christians. Most of them well dressed, respectable and had the appearance of being refined and educated, but there seemed to be representatives from almost every walk of life. While these people professed Christian truths in order to appease their consciences, they lived their lives in agreement with the powers of darkness. As they agreed with those powers, their assigned demons grew and more easily directed their actions.* (pg 13)

The Vision of the End Time Battle against the Church

In prayer, the Lord spoke to me that some of the greatest and most strategic battles that Satan will be waging against the Church in the coming days will be waged in the Church! He said the enemy will very often try to focus our attention on the outside, away from the Church. However, the Lord spoke to me that the most strategic battles of the demonic hordes will be fought from within the Church.

The weapons, agents, and seeds have already been planted in the midst of my people. To confirm the vision that Rick Joyner saw many years ago- Satan is going to use Christians as his primary weapons against the body of Christ. The so-called demonic powers will be riding on the back of many Christians as horses.

The Serpent is in the Garden!

I further enquired of the Lord to enlighten me on what He was speaking to me about. His reply was to take me to the Book of Beginnings, Genesis; the very accounts of man's fall!

In the garden, Man had everything that would make him live a fruitful and satisfying life! He was only to obey every of God's instructions to the letter! In this same beautiful garden was the reason for the fall; the serpent! The serpent that deceived our first mother and thus brought our fall – pain, shame, alienation from God, man and creation, was there in the garden! The enemy was within!

The Parable of the Wheat and the Tares (Matthew 13:24-29)

Jesus used many parables to illustrate His teachings – particularly teachings about the Kingdom! In one of His teachings about the difference between the present kingdom (where the sons of the kingdom and the sons of the evil one live together in human society), and the consummated kingdom (where there will be a distinction and separation), Jesus used the parable of the Wheat and the Tares.

Another parable He put forth to them, saying: "The kingdom of heaven is like a man who sowed good seed in his field; but while men slept, his enemy came and sowed tares among the wheat and went his way. But when the grain had sprouted and produced a crop, then the tares also appeared. So the servants of the owner came and said to him, 'Sir, did you not sow good seed in your field? How then does it have tares?' He said to them, 'An enemy has done this.' The servants said to him, 'Do you want us then to go and gather them up?' But he said, 'No, lest while you gather up the tares you also uproot the wheat with them."

Matthew 13:24 – 29 (NKJV)

For us to understand what Jesus was saying, it is important to identify what 'Tares' are!

Tares were very common in Palestine and closely resembled wheat; they are not really distinguishable from wheat until the grains appear at harvest time. In effect, what Jesus was trying to convey was that in the present kingdom of God – there will be both – sons of God and sons of the devil, and quite often, it will be very difficult if not impossible to differentiate them because they will be so similar!

The Wheat here represents the true sons of the kingdom, while the Tares represent children of darkness. Did you notice that they were both growing together side by side and so often they looked similar? What was Jesus trying to say to us?

THE ENEMY IS WITHIN!

Even the best of us, the most discerning of God's servants, may not be able to detect the difference. This is why He leaves the issue of 'Separation' to the very end and it will be carried out by the 'Holy Angels'

Are you downloading what the Spirit is saying to the Churches? The enemy is already in the camp! They will look, dress and talk like us – but they are still enemies of the cross of Christ.

The enemies that the Lord showed me have invaded the Church; they have been planted as Tares in the choir! Many of them are in the Elders' and Deacons' board! The Intercessory group has been infested with Tares, waiting for the opportune moment when the Church falls asleep; then they will strike.

I hear a call in the Spirit to the bride of Christ at this hour! Awake out of sleep! Wake up from your slumber! It's the season to pray, for if we will pray, we will stay. And if we will fast, we will last! There is a call for the bride of Christ to shake itself off from every spirit of slumber, apathy and lukewarm attitude.

As we prepare for the greatest battles of all ages, let's allow the famous song of George J Webb, 1803 – 1887, to rouse us to action.

1. Stand up, stand up for Jesus,
   Ye soldiers of the cross;
   Lift high his royal banner,
   It must not suffer loss.
   From victory unto victory
   His army shall he lead,
   Till every foe is vanquished,
   And Christ is Lord indeed.

2. Stand up, stand up for Jesus,
   The trumpet call obey;
   Forth to the mighty conflict,
   In this his glorious day.
   Ye that are brave now serve him
   Against unnumbered foes;
   Let courage rise with danger,
   And strength to strength oppose.

3. Stand up, stand up for Jesus,
   Stand in his strength alone;

The arm of flesh will fail you,
Ye dare not trust your own.
Put on the gospel armor,
Each piece put on with prayer;
Where duty calls or danger,
Be never wanting there.

4. Stand up, stand up for Jesus,
The strife will not be long;
This day the noise of battle,
The next the victor's song.
To him that overcometh,
A crown of life shall be;
They with the King of Glory
Shall reign eternally.

Appendices

STEPS TO SALVATION

- Admission and recognition that you are a sinner (Psalm 51:5)
- Repentance (1 John 1:9)
- Confession (Romans 10:9-10)
- Water and Holy Spirit baptism (Matthew 3: 6)
- Obedience to the Word of God (1 John 5:3)
- Fellowship with believers (Hebrews 10:25)

STEPS TO RECIEVING THE BAPTISM OF THE HOLY SPIRIT

- Understand that the Holy Spirit was poured out on the day of Pentecost (Acts 2:38)
- The born-again experience is the only qualification necessary for receiving the Holy Spirit baptism (Acts 2:38)
- The laying of hands is spiritual (Acts 18:7)
- Know what to expect (Acts 19:6)
- Disregard all fears about receiving a counterfeit for the Holy Spirit (Luke 11:11-13)

- Open your mouth as an act of faith to receive the Holy Spirit (Ephesians 5:18-19)
- Let all things be done decently and in order (1 Corinthians 14:33)

BECOME A COVENANT PARTNER WITH WORLD HARVEST CHRISTIAN CENTRE

There is power, fellowship and commitment in partnership, I invite you to become a partner with me in fulfilling the vision God has given me to teach and preach the word of Faith, Prosperity, Healing and Victorious Christian Living in order to complete the Great Commission.

To become a covenant Partner, simply fill out the appropriate information on the form overleaf and send it to our address today. I look forward to entering into a covenant relationship with you, and pray that the blessings of God will be manifested in your life.

My partners are valued friends and supporters of this ministry. I don't take lightly any responsibility to pray for you, diligently seek the word of God, and minister to you monthly in a personal letter. As an additional benefit of partnership, I will offer from time to time discounted products to you for your spiritual edification and growth.

COVENANT PARTNERSHIP FORM

I would like to become a covenant partner in prayer and financial support with World Harvest Christian Centre.

Name:

....

Address:

....P ost Code: ....

Tel No: ....

You can count on me for a monthly pledge of:

    £ 100.00 OR $ 100.00

    £ 50.00 $ 50.00

    £ 20.00 $ 20.00

    £ 10.00 $ 10.00

OR

A One off time gift of

£..............................

Signature: ....

PLEASE SEND TO:

World Harvest Christian Centre

25 – 27 Ruby Street

Old Kent Road

London

SE15 1LR

OTHER PUBLICATIONS BY PASTOR WALE BABATUNDE:

- Great Britain Has Fallen
- Awake Great Britain
- Parable of the Pound
- The Call of God
- Occupying Vacant Position
- Dreams: From Conception to Reality
- Wilderness Experience
- Pastoral Abuse
- Awake Canada
- Fulfilling Your Destiny
- You Can Plead for your case and Win

Copies available at your local bookstore, or contact:

World Harvest Christian Centre
25 – 27 Ruby Street
Old Kent Road
London
SE15 1LR
www.worldharvet.org.uk

Published by:Christian Heritage Publications

25 – 27 Ruby Street

London, SE15 1LR